Margret and H. A. Rey
Curious George®

CURIOUS ABOUT
PHONICS

12-STORY
LEARN-TO-READ
PROGRAM

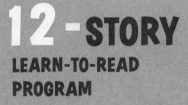

HOUGHTON MIFFLIN HARCOURT PUBLISHING COMPANY   BOSTON 2008

For information about permission to reproduce selections from this book, write to:
Permissions
Houghton Mifflin Harcourt Publishing Company
215 Park Avenue South
New York, NY 10003

Special Markets ISBN: 978-0-547-22339-1

www.hmhbooks.com

Printed in Singapore

TWP 10 9 8 7 6
4500321177

Margret and H. A. Rey's *Curious George*

CURIOUS ABOUT PHONICS LEARN-TO-READ PHONICS PROGRAM

Hello, parents! It is an exciting time—your curious child is ready to learn to read! George can help your child master some of the basic phonics skills that are the building blocks for a lifetime of reading and learning—and both of you can have fun doing it!

WHAT IS PHONICS? Phonics is a method of teaching children to read by helping them to associate written symbols (letters and groups of letters) with their corresponding sounds. Learning phonics will help your child to understand that the letters he or she sees on the page match up with the sounds we all say. Discovering basic phonics in the fun, low-stress context of the Curious George program will give your child the skills and confidence to move on and master higher-level reading, writing, and spelling skills.

HOW THE LEARN-TO-READ PHONICS PROGRAM WORKS: The program consists of twelve short stories set in the optimistic, playful world of Curious George. At the beginning of each story there are three sections containing information about that story. These sections are the following:

★ **New sounds in this book:** This section introduces the phonics sounds focused on in that story, for instance *short a, long o,* or *b,* along with an example of a word containing that sound.

★ **Here are some useful words you will see in this book. See how well you can learn them!** This section introduces several common words that appear in that story. These words, such as *the, and, but,* and so on, are so universal that it will be helpful if your child can recognize them early on. Many of these words (for example, *you* and *would*) do not follow the basic rules of phonics and therefore can pose a challenge to beginning readers. Even those that do follow the rules (for example, *it* and *with*) appear so frequently that stopping to work them out phonetically each time can slow a new reader to the point of frustration. By pointing out these common words and encouraging your child to memorize them, you will help him or her to read faster and understand more easily.

★**Here are some fun new words you will see in this book.** While most of the words are short and simple, there are a few longer words, too—PAJAMAS ALLIGATOR, DINOSAUR, and so on. These longer words, when presented in the context of the stories, help add interest to the stories and introduce your child to more difficult words in an engaging and manageable way.

USING THE PROGRAM

You are the most important part of making the learn-to-read phonics program a success! Here is what you can do to help your child learn to love reading—with a little help from Curious George.

★ **Find a quiet time to sit down with your child and the stories.**
★ **Encourage your child to ask questions and offer ideas and opinions.**
★ **Read through the first story. You can read it to your child the first time without stopping, to give him or her the flavor of the story. Or you can encourage your child to point out words he or she may already know as you read together. Be flexible and take a cue from your child's preferences in order to make the reading experience as engaging as possible.**
★ **Then go through the story again. This time, help your child find the key letters, useful words, and fun words. Help him or her sound out unfamiliar words, and talk about what is happening on each page.**
★ **Some children may want to read the first story again and again before moving on to the rest of the series. Others may prefer to read all the stories quickly and then return to the first. Again, don't hesitate to individualize the program to your child"s preferences. The best way to encourage a love of reading in your child is to make it fun and rewarding!**

SUGGESTIONS FOR FURTHER PHONICS FUN:

Look for the letters and words you've practiced in other places—on boxes in the pantry or at the grocery store, on billboards, on TV, or in newspaper headlines.

Talk about ideas found in the stories. For example, after reading #3, *Big and Little*, you could help your child spot other size comparisons in his or her own environment. After reading #6, *Let's Play*, you could ask your child to name additional ways he or she likes to play.

Extend the skills your child has learned from the program to other books. Try to find the time to read with him or her every day, and before you know it your child will be an independent reader!

Table of Contents

New sounds in this book:

short **a** as in **lap**
h as in **hold**

Here are some useful words
you will see in this book.
See how well you can learn them!

is   on   so

Here are some fun new words
you will see in this book.

rabbit   pancakes

Margret and H. A. Rey's
Curious George®

Curious About PHONICS
BOOK 1

CURIOUS GEORGE IS HAPPY

Written by Catherine Hapka

George
is happy.

He is happy
to pat a puppy.

He is happy
to chat with
a rabbit.

George is happy
to sit on a lap.

He is happy
to have
an apple.

George is
happy to try
on a hat.

He is happy
to have pancakes.

Sometimes George
is so happy that
he has to dance!

Margret and H. A. Rey's
Curious George®

Find out what makes Curious George happy, and learn about these sounds

short a   h

New sounds in this book:

short **e** as in **rest**

b as in **bike**

Here are some useful words
you will see in this book.
See how well you can learn them!

a   are

Here are some fun new words
you will see in this book.

bananas   presents

surprise   friend

Margret and H. A. Rey's

Curious George®

Curious About PHONICS
BOOK 2

THE BEST!

Written by Catherine Hapka

What does George like best?

He thinks
bananas are
the best
food ever.

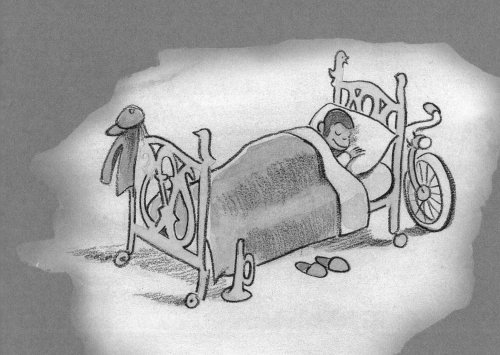

His bed is
the best place
to rest.

Presents are
the best kind
of surprise.

His best
present ever
was a bike.

Snow is the
best part
of winter.

Playing at
the beach is
the best part
of summer.

George loves his
friend best of all!

Margret and H. A. Rey's
Curious George®

Find out what Curious George likes the best, and learn about these sounds

short e   **b**

New sounds in this book:

short **a** as in **lap**
h as in **hold**

Here are some useful words
you will see in this book.
See how well you can learn them!

this   from   of

Here are some fun new words
you will see in this book.

**yellow   kitten   hippo
pajamas   window**

Margret and H. A. Rey's
Curious George®

Curious About PHONICS
BOOK 3

BIG AND LITTLE

Written by Catherine Hapka

The man
with the
yellow hat
is big.

George is
little.

This kitten
is little.

This hippo is big.

This blue fish is little.

This yellow fish is big.

Wow! This gift is big!

This ship is even bigger!

These pajamas
are way too big!

This stack of dishes
is big.

George wishes
it were little.

What does George see from the window?

It's a big bunch of kids!
Come on in!

Margret and H. A. Rey's
Curious George®

Compare sizes with Curious George, and learn about these sounds:

short i   w

New sounds in this book:

short **O** as in **not**

d as in **doctor**

**Here are some useful words
you will see in this book.
See how well you can learn them!**

why   no   at

**Here are some fun new words
you will see in this book.**

**hospital   problem
doctor   lollipop**

Margret and H. A. Rey's
Curious George

Curious About PHONICS
BOOK 4

THE DOCTOR'S OFFICE

Written by Catherine Hapka

Why is George at the hospital?

Is something wrong?

No problem!
He's just
visiting the
doctor's office.

The doctor will see you now!

The doctor
helps George's
body stay well.

George does
NOT like
getting his
shots!

After his shots,
George gets a
lollipop.

See you next
year, Doc!

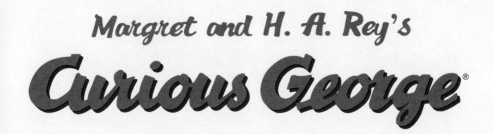

Margret and H. A. Rey's

Curious George®

Go to the doctor's office with Curious George, and learn about these sounds:

short o   **d**

New sounds in this book:

short **u** as in **fun**

j as in **jump**

Here are some useful words
you will see in this book.
See how well you can learn them!

how it your

Here are some fun new words
you will see in this book.

juggle tumble curious

Margret and H. A. Rey's

Curious About PHONICS
BOOK 5

Curious George®

FUN, FUN, FUN

Written by Catherine Hapka

How does George have fun?

It is fun
to juggle.

A drum
is fun!

It is fun
to jump.

It is just as
much fun
to tumble.

It is fun
to fill
your
tummy.

A bug!
What fun!

It is fun to
be curious!

Margret and H. A. Rey's Curious George®

Find out how Curious George has fun, and learn about these sounds:

short u   j

New sounds in this book:

long **a** as in **way**
p as in **pail**

Here are some useful words
you will see in this book.
See how well you can learn them!

and   with   will

Here are some fun new words
you will see in this book.

baseball spade alligator

Margret and H. A. Rey's
Curious George®

Curious About PHONICS
BOOK 6

LET'S PLAY!

Written by Catherine Hapka

George
wants
to play.

What will he play today?

He could
play a
game.

He could
play with
a train.

How about baseball?

He could play
with his pail
and spade.

Should he play with an alligator?

No way!
Run away!

Will you play with George?

Margret and H. A. Rey's

Curious George®

Play all day with Curious George, and learn about these sounds:

long a   p

New sounds in this book:

long e as in see
t as in take

Here are some useful words
you will see in this book.
See how well you can learn them!

some   done   not

Here are some fun new words
you will see in this book.

**job yippee
careful happier**

Margret and H. A. Rey's
Curious George®

SEE GEORGE TAKE A JOB

Written by Catherine Hapka

See George
take a job.

George will clean today.

What does
George see?

George sees some green paint.
How neat!

See what George
has done! Yippee!

George flees!

114

Whee!
Be careful,
George!

George does
not need a job.
He is happier
in a tree!

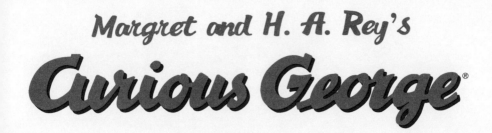

Margret and H. A. Rey's

Curious George®

Take a job with Curious George, and
learn about these sounds:

long e   t

New sounds in this book:

long **i** as in **kite**

I as in **like**

Here are some useful words
you will see in this book.
See how well you can learn them!

for   does   what

Here are some fun new words
you will see in this book.

dinosaurs   library

Margret and H. A. Rey's
Curious George®

WHAT DOES
GEORGE LIKE?

Written by Catherine Hapka

What does George like?

He likes
to ride a
bike.

He likes dinosaurs.

He likes
to hike.

He likes
the library.

He likes
ice cream.

He likes to fly a kite.

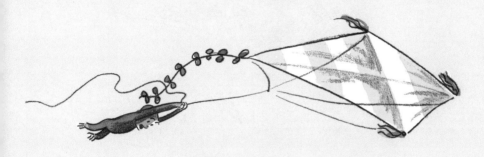

Yikes!

George likes to
go for a drive.
How nice!

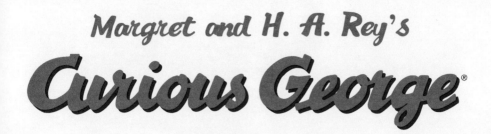

Margret and H. A. Rey's

Curious George®

Find out what Curious George likes, and learn about these sounds:

long i l

New sounds in this book:

long **O** as in **snow**
S as in **slow**

Here are some useful words
you will see in this book.
See how well you can learn them!

yes   go   be

Here are some fun new words
you will see in this book.

snow   sled

Margret and H. A. Rey's
Curious George

Curious About PHONICS
BOOK 9

SNOW

Written by Catherine Hapka

George
likes snow.

George
wants
to go.

Is the
sled slow?

No!

Slower,
George!
Slower!

Uh-oh . . .

Will George be okay?

Yes!

Way to go,
George!

Margret and H. A. Rey's

Curious George®

Spend a day in the snow with Curious George, and learn about these sounds:

long o   **s**

New sounds in this book:

long **u** as in **huge**
c as in **cute**

Here are some useful words
you will see in this book.
See how well you can learn them!

you   one   in

Here are some fun new words
you will see in this book.

costume   ghost   spooky

Margret and H. A. Rey's
Curious George®

COSTUMES

Written by Catherine Hapka

George is
going to a
costume party.

What will
he wear?

What do you
think of this
space suit?

This one
is cute.
But it's
too small.

This costume
is huge!

This tutu
might look
better in blue.

Ooh! What
big boots!

A ghost
costume is
too spooky!

Aha! George found a super cowboy costume.

Yee-haw, dude!

Margret and H. A. Rey's

Curious George®

Try on costumes with Curious George, and learn about these sounds:

long u   c

New sounds in this book:

plural final **S** as in **books**

f as in **four**

**Here are some useful words
you will see in this book.
See how well you can learn them!**

he to has

**Here are some fun new words
you will see in this book.**

**kangaroos camels
flowers balloons penguins**

Margret and H. A. Rey's Curious George

HOW MANY?

Written by Catherine Hapka

Help George
count to ten!

George has one banana.

George meets
two kangaroos.

He sees
three camels.

George has
four books.

He sees five lollipops.

George counts
six flowers.

George has
seven yellow
hats.

George grabs
eight balloons.

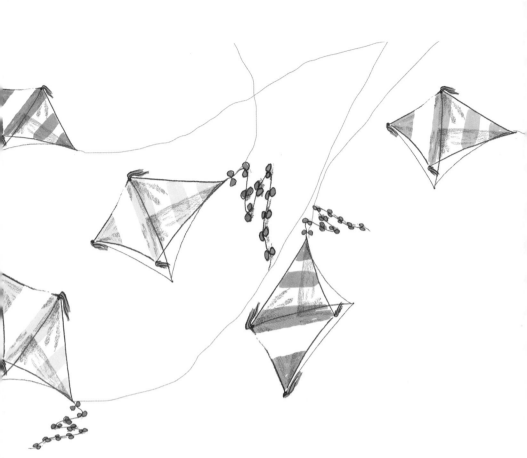

George
spies nine fine
kites.

George dances with ten funny penguins.

One to ten—that's the end!

Margret and H. A. Rey's
Curious George®

Count to ten with Curious George, and learn about these sounds:

final s   f

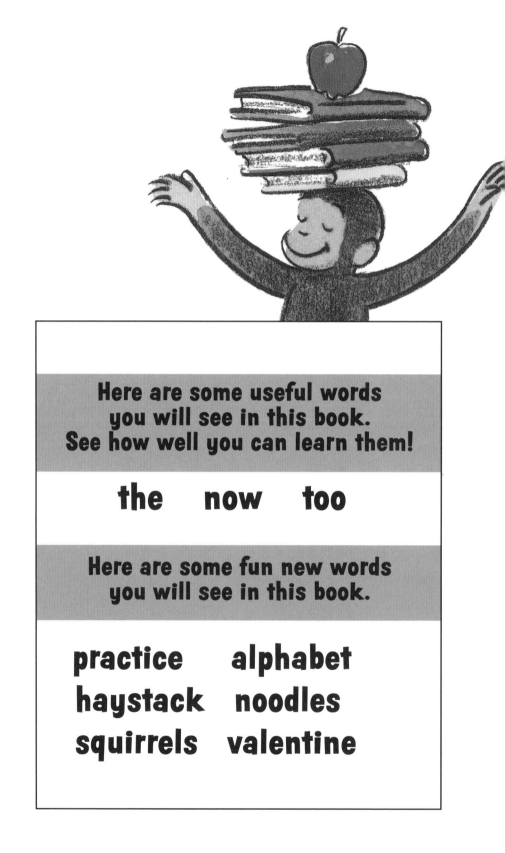

Here are some useful words
you will see in this book.
See how well you can learn them!

the   now   too

Here are some fun new words
you will see in this book.

practice   alphabet
haystack   noodles
squirrels   valentine

Margret and H. A. Rey's
Curious George®

Curious About PHONICS
BOOK 12

FROM ABC TO XYZ

Written by Catherine Hapka

Help George practice the alphabet!

Apple

Birthday **C**ake
with candles

Dog at the door

Eggs

Flowers

George going fishing

Haystack

Ice cream cone

Jar

Kite

Library

Messy Noodles, Oh, my!

Pancakes

Quick little squirrels

Record player

Sled

Trunk full of costumes

Uh-oh!
Too big!

Valentine

Wave
goodbye

X
marks
the spot

Y o-yo

Zigzag

George is so
proud to know
all his letters—
just like you!